SNOOPY, TOP DOG

Selected cartoons from
THE BEAGLE HAS LANDED
Volume 2

by CHARLES M. SCHULZ

FAWCETT CREST • NEW YORK

SNOOPY, TOP DOG

This book, prepared especially for Fawcett Crest Books, a unit of CBS Publications, the Consumer Publishing Division of CBS Inc., comprises a portion of THE BEAGLE HAS LANDED and is reprinted by arrangement with Holt, Rinehart and Winston, Inc.

Contents of Book: PEANUTS* comic strips by
                            Charles M. Schulz
                            Copyright © 1977 United Feature
                            Syndicate, Inc.

ISBN: 0-449-24373-7

Printed in the United States of America

First Fawcett Crest Printing: February 1981

10 9 8 7 6 5 4 3 2

SNOOPY, TOP DOG

HALF?!

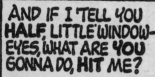

WHY SHOULD WE GIVE YOU HALF OF OUR MONEY? TEN PERCENT IS ALL YOU DESERVE!

AND IF I TELL YOU HALF, LITTLE WINDOW-EYES, WHAT ARE YOU GONNA DO, HIT ME?

NO, I AM!!

POW!

War and
Punishment

Crime and
Peace

※WHEW※ I DON'T KNOW WHAT'S WRONG WITH ME LATELY...

I WALK ABOUT ONE BLOCK, AND I GET SO WEAK I CAN HARDLY DRAG THIS BLANKET...

NO PROBLEM, MANAGER..
I MISSED IT, BUT THE
GROUND CAUGHT IT!

NICE CATCH, GROUND!
YOU'RE DOING A
GOOD JOB!

I NEVER REALIZED
THE GROUND WAS
ON OUR SIDE...

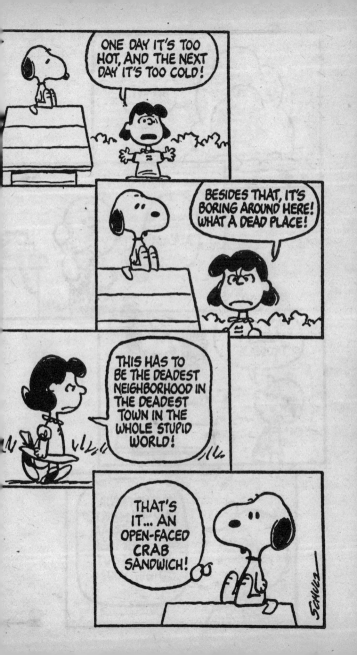

ARE YOU ALL SET TO GO?

IF YOU'RE GOING TO BE PEPPERMINT PATTY'S WATCHDOG, YOU'D BETTER TAKE ALONG A WEAPON

THAT'S A GOOD IDEA... I'LL TAKE ALONG THE MOST DANGEROUS WEAPON EVER DEVISED BY MAN!

HI, SNOOPY... I APPRECIATE YOUR COMING OVER...

I GUESS CHUCK TOLD YOU THAT MY DAD'S OUT OF TOWN, AND I HATE STAYING ALONE

WHAT'S THE HOCKEY STICK FOR? YOU CAN'T GUARD OUR HOUSE WITH A HOCKEY STICK...

I COULD GET MUGGED WHILE YOU'RE SITTING IN THE PENALTY BOX!

SIGH

IT'S A GOOD FEELING KNOWING THERE'S A WATCHDOG OUTSIDE

ESPECIALLY WHEN YOU KNOW HE'S ROUGH AND TOUGH...

THIS IS THE FIRST NEEDLEPOINT I'VE TRIED WITH PICTURES OF BUNNIES...

CHUCK, YOU GET OVER HERE RIGHT AWAY!

SNOOPY WAS YOUR RESPONSIBILITY! IF HE'S RUN OUT ON ME, YOU'RE GONNA TAKE HIS PLACE!

YOU'RE GONNA BE THE WATCHDOG, CHUCK! DO YOU HEAR ME?!

WOOF!

YOU SURE TOOK YOUR SWEET TIME GETTING OVER HERE, CHUCK

I COULD HAVE BEEN MUGGED TWENTY TIMES BY NOW! ANYWAY, SNOOPY LEFT SO YOU HAVE TO BE MY WATCHDOG...

I'LL BE YOUR WATCHDOG, AND I'LL SIT OUT HERE ON THE PORCH, BUT I WON'T WEAR **THAT**!

OKAY, CHUCK, WE'LL FORGET THE COLLAR

OKAY, WATCHDOG, YOU CAN WAKE UP.. IT'S MORNING!

WOW! THAT WAS A LONG NIGHT...I DON'T THINK I'D MAKE A GOOD WATCHDOG...

SNOOPY! WHERE HAVE YOU BEEN?

AROUND THE WORLD AND BACK! I'M IN LOVE!!

THE WEDDING WILL TAKE PLACE HERE IN THE BACKYARD

THE BRIDE WILL ENTER THROUGH THAT SMALL GATE...SNOOPY AND SPIKE WILL STAND OVER THERE

THE RECEPTION WILL BE HELD DOWNSTAIRS IN THE DOGHOUSE

I'M HAVING THE RECREATION ROOM DONE OVER IN PINK AND WHITE

ALL RIGHT, HERE'S THE GROOM! WHERE'S THE BRIDE AND THE BEST MAN?

I'VE GOT SOME GOOD NEWS FOR YOU AND SOME BAD NEWS...

THE GOOD NEWS IS THAT THE BRIDE AND THE BEST MAN ARE HERE

THE BAD NEWS IS THEY JUST RAN OFF TOGETHER!

KLUNK!

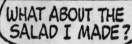

I'M WORRIED THAT I MIGHT GROW UP TO BE A DITCH DIGGER...

WELL, THAT COULD HAPPEN...

BUT MAYBE LATER ON YOU COULD DO SOMETHING ELSE

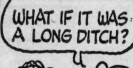

WHAT IF IT WAS A LONG DITCH?

THE GIRLS AND I HAVE FORMED A CLUB

THAT'S NICE...CLUBS CAN BE FUN...

WE DECIDED TO HOLD OUR ANNUAL MEETING ONCE A YEAR...

DON'T YOU WANT TO HEAR WHAT ELSE WE DECIDED?

SCHULZ

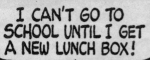

"MY SUMMER VACATION"

THIS SUMMER I VISITED MY GRANDFATHER'S RANCH.. WELL, I GUESS IT ISN'T EXACTLY A RANCH...

HE LIVES SORT OF IN THE COUNTRY...KIND OF ON THE EDGE OF TOWN...

ACTUALLY, HE HAS AN APARTMENT OVER A DRUG STORE!

SCHULZ

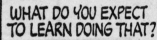

INSTEAD OF WATCHING TV YOU SHOULD BE READING A BOOK!

INSTEAD OF WATCHING TV YOU COULD BE STRAIGHTENING UP YOUR ROOM!

INSTEAD OF WATCHING TV YOU COULD EVEN BE PLAYING OUTSIDE!

THERE'S A LOT MORE TO LIFE THAN NOT WATCHING TV!

THIS IS THE TIME OF YEAR WHEN SOME OF THE LEAVES BEGIN TO FALL...

KLUNK

NOT THE BIRDS... JUST THE LEAVES!

I'VE DECIDED I DON'T WANT TO KICK IT

WHY NOT?

WHAT DID IT EVER DO TO ME?

"I can't tell you how much I love you," he said.

"Try," she said.

"I'm very fond of you," he said.

"Nice try," she said.

MORE PEANUTS®

(in editions with brightly colored pages)

☐ A BOY NAMED CHARLIE BROWN   23217 $2.25

☐ SNOOPY AND HIS SOPWITH CAMEL   23799 $1.75

☐ SNOOPY AND THE RED BARON   23719 $1.75

☐ THE "SNOOPY, COME HOME"
    MOVIE BOOK   23726 $1.95